Marco Polo

Jennifer Strand

abdopublishing.com

Published by Abdo Zoom™, PO Box 398166, Minneapolis, Minnesota 55439. Copyright © 2017 by Abdo Consulting Group, Inc. International copyrights reserved in all countries. No part of this book may be reproduced in any form without written permission from the publisher. Abdo Zoom™ is a trademark and logo of Abdo Consulting Group, Inc.

Printed in the United States of America, North Mankato, Minnesota
072016
092016

Cover Photo: Hulton-Deutsch/Hulton-Deutsch Collection/Corbis
Interior Photos: Hulton-Deutsch/Hulton-Deutsch Collection/Corbis, 1; North Wind Picture Archives, 4, 8, 9, 10–11, 14, 16, 19; Nateethep Ratanavipanon/Shutterstock Images, 4–5; Canaletto/Library of Congress, 6–7; Stock Montage/Getty Images, 7; Dea Picture Library/De Agostini/Getty Images, 12–13; Rudyanto Wijaya/iStockphoto, 13; Blue Sky Studio/Shutterstock Images, 15; Leemage/UIG/Getty Images, 17; Yuri Yavnik/Shutterstock Images, 18–19

Editor: Emily Temple
Series Designer: Madeline Berger
Art Direction: Dorothy Toth

Publisher's Cataloging-in-Publication Data
Names: Strand, Jennifer, author.
Title: Marco Polo / by Jennifer Strand.
Description: Minneapolis, MN : Abdo Zoom, [2017] | Series: Pioneering
     explorers | Includes bibliographical references and index.
Identifiers: LCCN 2016941520 | ISBN 9781680792454 (lib. bdg.) |
     ISBN 9781680794137 (ebook) | 9781680795028 (Read-to-me ebook)
Subjects: LCSH: Polo, Marco, 1254-1323?--Juvenile literature. | Explorers--
     Italy--Biography--Juvenile literature. | Travel, Medieval--Juvenile literature.
Classification: DDC 915.042/2/092 [B]--dc23
LC record available at http://lccn.loc.gov/2016941520

Table of Contents

Introduction

Marco Polo was an explorer.

Colvin, Nancy B

44729

Friday, February 25, 2022

31183183533030   Marco Polo

He wrote a book about traveling to Asia. He was not the first European to go to Asia. But his book made him famous.

5

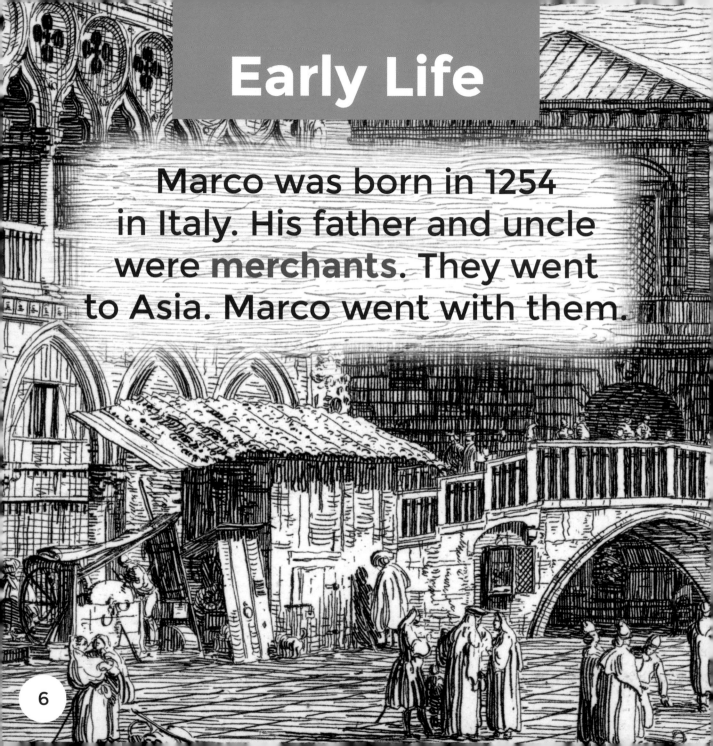

Early Life

Marco was born in 1254 in Italy. His father and uncle were **merchants**. They went to Asia. Marco went with them.

6

The journey took four years.

China was part of
the Mongol **Empire**.

Kublai Khan was its leader.
Polo worked for him.

Polo went many places in Asia.
He learned about the way
people lived there.

Then he went
back to Italy.

History Maker

Polo told stories about Asia to a writer. They made a book.

It was called
The Travels of Marco Polo.

The book told what he saw in Asia.
It was **popular**.

But many people did not believe the stories.

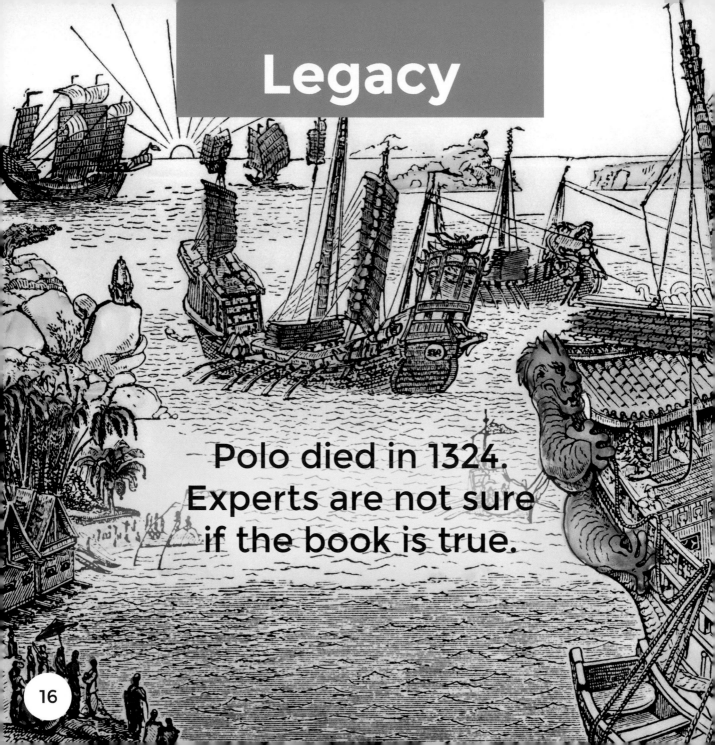

Legacy

Polo died in 1324.
Experts are not sure
if the book is true.

Some think he did not
go to China.

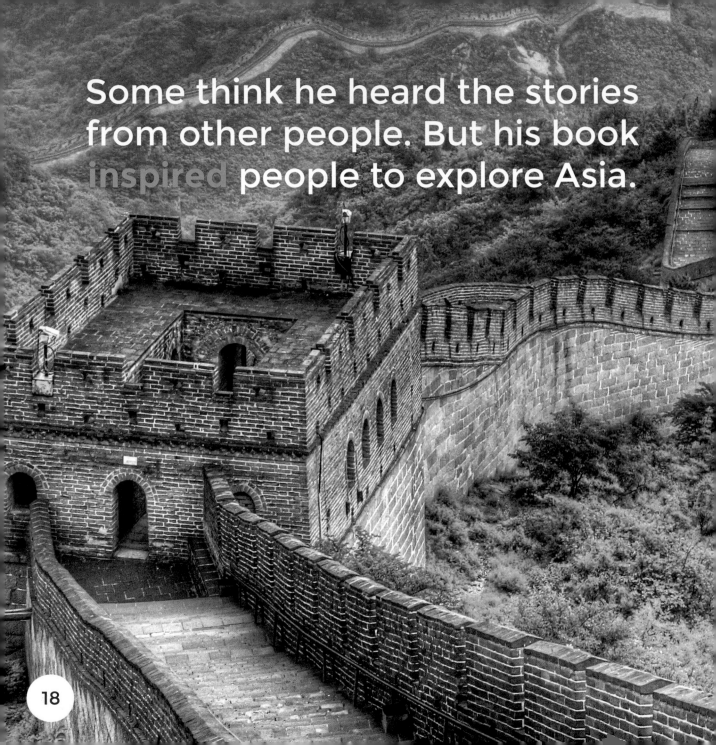

Some think he heard the stories from other people. But his book inspired people to explore Asia.

Marco Polo

Born: 1254

Birthplace: Venice, Italy

Wife: Donata Badoer

Known For: Polo traveled to Asia. His book *The Travels of Marco Polo* told about his adventures.

Died: January 8 or 9, 1324

Key Dates

1254: Marco Polo is born.

1271-1274: Polo travels to China with his father and uncle.

1274-1292: Polo works for Kublai Khan. He goes to many parts of Asia.

1295: Polo arrives back in Venice, Italy.

1300: Polo's book, *The Travels of Marco Polo,* is published.

1324: Polo dies in January.

Glossary

empire - a large group of people and land that is controlled by one ruler.

explorer - a person who travels to new places.

inspired - encouraged or influenced others.

merchant - someone who sells things to make money.

popular - liked or enjoyed by many people.

Booklinks

For more information
on **Marco Polo**, please visit
booklinks.abdopublishing.com

 **In on Biographies!**

Learn even more with the Abdo Zoom
Biographies database. Check out
abdozoom.com for more information.

Index